Evaluate Yourself
Brain Power

Evaluate Yourself
Brain Power

(Expert guidance to help you use your intelligence to the optimum)

Contributors
Jane Sherrod Singer
Dr. C.C. Thurston

Compiled and Edited by
Vijaya Kumar

A Sterling Paperback

STERLING PAPERBACKS
An imprint of
Sterling Publishers (P) Ltd.
A-59, Okhla Industrial Area, Phase-II,
New Delhi-110020.
Tel: 26387070, 26386209; Fax: 91-11-26383788
E-mail: sterlingpublishers@airtelbroadband.in
ghai@nde.vsnl.net.in
www.sterlingpublishers.com

Evaluate Yourself: Brain Power
© 1998, Sterling Publishers (P) Ltd.
ISBN 81 207 1987 5
Originally Published under the title: Let's get Quizzical, Marriage
Reprint 2004, 2006, 2007

Quiz Material – Courtesy, Singer Media Corporation, California

All rights are reserved.
No part of this publication may be reproduced, stored in a retrieval system or transmitted, in any form or by any means, mechanical, photocopying, recording or otherwise, without prior written permission of the original publisher.

Printed and Published by Sterling Publishers Pvt. Ltd., New Delhi-110 020.

Editor's Word

During this restless period in history, we talk about Black Power, Green Power, Man Power, and yet we seldom consider one factor which we all possess — Brain Power. The muscles of the body can be strengthened by exercises. The same is true of the mind. Studies prove conclusively that one's native intelligence can be increased with study and concentration.

This quiz book will help you determine whether or not you are using to your optimum those little grey cells housed in your brainbox.

Contents

	Editor's Word	v
1.	Can you think sequentially?	1
2.	Are you pushing your I.Q.?	4
3.	Are you a quick-wit?	7
4.	Do you have an inquiring mind?	12
5.	Can you look ahead?	16
6.	Can you make a fast decision?	19
7.	Would you be a good detective?	22
8.	Would you be a good witness?	26
9.	Do you have an orderly mind?	30
10.	How well do you concentrate?	34
11.	How good is your judgement?	37
12.	How well do you judge people?	41
13.	Can you think ahead?	44
14.	Do you have ESP?	47
15.	Can you untangle problems?	50
16.	Are you logical?	54
17.	Do you think logically?	57
18.	Are you ingenious?	60
19.	How creative are you?	63
20.	Are you observant?	67
21.	How good is your visual memory?	72

22.	Can you follow directions?	79
23.	Can you solve problems?	82
24.	How fast can you see things?	86
25.	Do you see details?	91
26.	Are you sharp-witted?	94
27.	Can you think in 3 dimensions?	97
28.	How great is your brain power?	101
29.	Do you use your brain power?	105
30.	Can you identify forms?	109

Can You Think Sequentially? ⟦1⟧

Most of us have to borrow the worn phrase, put "the cart before the horse", because we did not think through a situation, step by step, in its logical sequence. We have perhaps painted ourselves into a corner, had to rip apart a dress we were making or disassemble a machine we were repairing, and start over. The ability to think sequentially shows a kind of intelligence but not all intelligent people are capable of assembling a satisfactory sequential chain of reasoning.

Tackle these questions.
1. Supply the missing number:
   4   12   36   108   _____
2. If a man was first a boy, and a woman was first a girl, then
   a) a cat was first a _____.
   b) a dog was first a _____.
3. Some riddles are tests of sequential thinking. Try this very old one:
   > As I was going to St. Ives
   > I met a group of seven wives.
   > Every wife had seven sacks;
   > Every sack had seven kittens
   > Kittens, cats, sacks and wives,
   > How many were going to St. Ives?
4. Supply the missing number:
   5   1   5
   6   2   12
   3   4   ?
5. Put these words in a sensible sequence:
   a) PENNY   DOLLAR   DIME
      HALF-DOLLAR   NICKLE   QUARTER
   b) FOOT   WAIST   SHOULDER
      CHEST   KNEE   NECK
      ANKLE   HEAD   CALF
      THIGH

Answers
1. 324 (Each number in the sequence is multiplied by 3) 10 points

2. 1. Kitten, 2. Puppy (2 points each)
3. One person was going to St. Ives — myself (5 points)
4. 12 (In each row, reading across, the number in the last column is found by multiplying the first two numbers.) (10 points)
5. 1. SEED, SAPLING, LEAVES,
      (or the reverse order)   (5 points)
   2. FOOT, ANKLE, CALF, KNEE, THIGH, WAIST, CHEST, SHOULDER, NECK, HEAD
      (or the reverse order)   (6 points)

ANALYSIS

31-40: Provided you stayed within the time limit, this is an excellent score. You put "first things first". It is very unlikely that you hange the clothing you wear every day behind those which you seldom wear. When you plan a trip, your luggage is packed so the things you will need first are readily at hand. Your home/office is well-organised.

20-30: This is an average and a good score. Occasionally, as most of us, you get the "cart before the horse!" But most of the time you have a good sense of sequential logic.

10-19: Probably you never took the time to think about the need for step-by-step procedures. Your attitude could easily be one of fun and a bit random.

0-9: This is a low score, but one which can easily be improved.

2

Are You Pushing Your I.Q.?

> *It is a fact that one's intelligence can be expanded by tests and exercises just as one's muscles respond to activity. As the German dramatist and poet, Johann Schiller, observed: "Intellect is brain force." This test will challenge the grey cells in your head.*

1. Which of the five animals is least like the other four?
   A. Cow _____
   B. Giraffe _____
   C. Deer _____
   D. Dog _____
   E. Bird _____
2. If you rearrange the letters of CWO, you would have the name of an:
   A. Animal _____
   B. Automobile _____
   C. Ocean _____
3. Which word below logically fits into this statement: *Hat* is to *Head* as *Shoe* is to _____.
   A. Arm _____
   B. Hair _____
   C. Foot _____
   D. Eyes _____
4. Which of the words below is the opposite of *Asleep*?
   A. Daytime _____
   B. Live _____
   C. Awake _____
5. A farmer took a basket of eggs to town. He sold 1/3 of the eggs at one store. Then he sold 2/3 of the remainder at another store. Then he found he had two dozen eggs left. How many eggs did he have at the beginning?
   A. 54 eggs _____
   B. 24 eggs _____
   C. 144 eggs _____

Answers and Scoring

1. E (The other animals have four feet. Only the bird can fly—20 points)
2. A (If the letters are rearranged properly the word is COW which is an animal—20 points)
3. C (You put your hat on your head and a shoe on your foot—20 points)

4. C—20 points
5. A—80 points

ANALYSIS

80-100: Testees in this range usually push their I.Q. They are observant and mentally alert.

40-60: The people who rate this score often like to be told. However, with a bit of stimulus, they increase their ability to think with incredible speed.

0-20: This is a weak score. Check back on the answers and try this test again.

Are You A Quick-Wit?

3

> *In this fast-moving world you have to be quick-witted. It's to the fleetest of mind that progress goes.*
>
> *So, have you got your wits about you? Are you alert, able to make the right decisions quickly?*
>
> *In this quiz series, the questions, different though they might appear, are all designed to test your speed of thought and action. Are you a real quick-wit? Well, we'll see!*

Answer these questions.
1. You're in a railway compartment when a fellow passenger has a heart attack. Do you
    a) Pull the communication cord at once?
    b) Let the train continue and go find the guard?
    c) Allow the train to go on, but go along the corridor asking if there's a doctor?
2. You enter a room to find a young child out on the window ledge in a precarious position. Do you
    a) Call softly to it?
    b) Rush forward and try to grab it?
    c) Try and creep up on it quietly?
3. Which of these words is different from the others? (four can be prefixed by one word, the other cannot.)
    a) window   b) beans   c) pavement
    d) polish   e) poodle
4. What would you sooner have as a *long-term* investment, assuming that you merely stacked them away in a draw?
    a) 1,000 in cash
    b) 1,000 in diamonds
    c) 1,000 in gold
5. You're on a bicycle when you see four bank robbers jump into a car. You notice their vehicle has a puncture and that there would be a fair chance of catching them on your bike. Do you
    a) Chase after them at once?
    b) Stop a car and ask the driver to give chase?
    c) Just take the number and phone it to the police?

6. Which is the missing animal:
   DON + (door opener) = (animal)
7. You are shipwrecked on a desert island. Which of these things would you sooner have with you at the time?
   a) A shotgun, ammunition and spade?
   b) A three-year supply of canned food?
   c) A small boat?
8. You're near an electric railway when you see a man lying across the live line; there is a telephone box nearby. Do you
   a) Try and shift him?
   b) Telephone the police and then go back to the spot?
   c) Try to telephone the railway?

Now look below for the answers you should have ticked and for the verdict on your quick-wittedness!

ANSWERS

Give yourself just three points for every one you've got right.

1. (c) is the right answer. If you pulled the alarm cord, you would stop the train; there might be medical help available at the next station. The best thing is to go along the train looking for medical help.... eventually you would come to the guard anyway.
2. (a) is right this time. Either of the other two alternatives would undoubtedly startle the child and this could make it fall.
3. (e) is the right answer. *Pavement* is different from the four other words. They can be prefixed by the word "french", pavement cannot.
4. (b) 1,000 in diamonds. Diamonds seem to keep their value much better than the other two alternatives.

5. (c) is right. What would you do even if you caught up with them on your bicycle or in another car? You would be outnumbered and the robbers would most likely escape just the same. Better to let the police know and they can get their cars looking for the number quickly.
6. Don + (key) = Donkey.
7. (a) seems right. With a shotgun, ammunition and spade you could probably survive longer than the three years which the food would last you. Taking the boat is a complete shot in the dark—you're better off on the island.
8. (b) is right. If you tried to shift him you would probably only electrocute yourself as well. The big thing is to stop any train running over him... and if you phone the police they would see to this (by warning the railway) and also to getting medical help there quickly. If you tried phoning the railway you might have trouble finding the right person and you would not be covering the medical side. By phoning the police and then going back to look out for oncoming trains you would take the best course available to you.

ANALYSIS

Between 18 and 24: You're very quick witted indeed. You've learnt that being quick-witted does not always entail jumping quickly into action on the first thought that comes into your head. You've learnt that, in the long run, it is better to spend a little time on thought before taking action. You're a sharp one in any circumstances.

Between 9 and 15: You're quite quick-witted at times, but you're inclined to jump quickly into action; your reaction is good but sometimes you take longer to get results simply because you haven't allowed a little time for thought.

Under 6: Sorry, a lot of sharpening-up needed here. You don't use your wits enough.

Do You Have An Inquiring Mind?

> *To the despair of many parents, babies and children are insatiably inquisitive. To the despair of teachers, many young people, as they grow older, lose this desire to discover, to investigate, to learn new things. This test will help you assess whether or not you have "turned off" your naturally inquiring mind.*

Please pick the answer nearest your own in the following situations.
1. I have a broken alarm clock. I will
   a) Take it apart and try to fix it
   b) Have it repaired
   c) Throw it away.
2. When I see a fence around a building that is being erected, I
   a) Look for an opening in the fence so I can see what is going on
   b) Couldn't care less
   c) Ask somebody what is being built.
3. When new products are brought out on the market, I
   a) Stick to my old tried-and-true materials
   b) Try them immediately.
   c) Wait until I talk with someone who has tried them.
4. In my community a course in ecology will be given. Provided I have time, I will
   a) Ignore it
   b) Investigate the subject and attend the first lecture as a test
   c) Take the full course whether I like it or not.
5. There is a zoo in my community. I
   a) Could spend hours observing the animals
   b) Have more important things to do
   c) Go when friends, especially children, ask me to.
6. When I ask questions, I
   a) Usually want to know the reason "why" for things

b) Usually want to know details, such as "what", "who" or "when"
   c) Am cautious because I don't want to sound stupid.
7. When at a party, I
   a) Stay near my friends
   b) Get involved with those who introduce themselves to me
   c) Am almost automatically drawn toward strangers.
8. When I see a plane or a ship leaving for foreign countries, I
   a) Have a great urge to be on it
   b) Am glad I have my home to return to
   c) Trace its route on a map.
9. When there is a "happening" nearby, such as a fair, home-and-garden show, or automobile exhibit, I
   a) Read about it in the paper
   b) Make every effort to attend
   c) Am basically disinterested.

SCORING FOR ANSWERS
1. A — 10, B — 5,   C — 0
2. A — 10, B — 0,   C — 5
3. A — 0,   B — 10, C — 5
4. A — 0,   B — 8,   C — 10
5. A — 10, B — 0,   C — 5
6. A — 10, B — 8,   C — 0
7. A — 0,   B — 5,   C — 10
8. A — 10, B — 0,   C — 5
9. A — 5,   B — 10, C — 0

YOUR SCORE
60-80: Those in this scoring bracket have an inquisitive nature. In some cases, led by their curiosity, they tend to go in too many directions. If they evaluate the worth and

importance of their investigations and put the information to use, they have an interesting and productive life. They may wear out their families and friends but they never bore them.

30-50: This score is usually rated by practical people who are quite satisfied with the way things are and the information they have at hand.

0-25: People in this scoring range are often bored with themselves and their lives. They have lost interest in exploring new vistas.

Can You Look Ahead?

5

> *It has been wisely said: "To be forewarned is to be forearmed." The statement is very true, and the ability to look ahead, plan ahead and think ahead requires great talent. Fortunately, this personality quality can be trained if a person wishes to increase his skill. This test will give you some hints about your own practical approach to life and your ability to make plans for the future.*

Answer Yes or No.
1. Discounting emergencies, are you usually without overdue bills?
   Yes_____   No_____
2. Do you plan your day's activities in advance?
   Yes_____   No_____
3. Do you usually make notes and lists, and jot down reminders?
   Yes_____   No_____
4. Do your friends and associates usually react to your suggestions as you expect them to?
   Yes_____   No_____
5. Are you usually dressed appropriately for the weather or for the special occasion?
   Yes_____   No_____
6. Do you sincerely try to understand the motivations of your friends, family and associates?
   Yes_____   No_____
7. When you have succeeded or failed, do you try to evaluate the reasons why?
   Yes_____   No_____
8. For special occasions, such as a holiday or birthday, do you often have to rush out to do "last minute" shopping for someone you've overlooked?
   Yes_____   No_____
9. Do you often find in doing a project at home, on the job or in school, that you have neglected to buy, bring or have the necessary tools?
   Yes_____   No_____

Answers

Give yourself 10 points each for the following:
1. Yes. 2. Yes 3. Yes 4. Yes
6. Yes 7. Yes 8. No 9. No.

Your Score

70-90: This is an excellent score! Those who rate this high are seldom surprised by the daily routine or even by emergencies because they are well organised and have looked ahead.

40-60: This is an average score. Most testees, when questioned further agreed: "Most of the time I do look ahead but I often get distracted by details and forget to think about the next step."

0-30: This is a weak score but one which can easily be improved. Life will be much easier for those who evaluate the reasons why they missed on certain questions, and try to make the necessary adjustments in day-to-day living.

Can You Make A Fast Decision? [6]

> *It has been said: "He who hesitates is lost." But humorist James Thurber quipped: "He who hesitates is sometimes saved." Life requires that we take time to evaluate in many decisions such as marriage, financial matters and our future. Then there are daily events which demand a fast decision, a matter of life or death, a quick answer on a job. This test will help you assess the speed at which you are able to reach a decision.*

Choose an option from each.
1. You have just bought a very expensive car. On your way home the car stalls on a railroad track and you are faced with a fast oncoming freight train. You would:
   a) Stay in your new car and try to get it started.
   b) Leap from the car.
   c) Freeze from fear.
2. A stranger has cut his wrist badly, is losing blood rapidly and is in a state of shock. You would:
   a) Look for a telephone and call a doctor.
   b) Summon the police.
   c) Try to restrict the flow of blood above the wrist.
3. A friend asks you to join him tomorrow on a short vacation. You have both the time and money and are not needed by your family. You want to make the trip. You would:
   a) Start packing immediately.
   b) Refuse to join him since it is too much of a spur-of-the-moment invitation.
   c) Say you will think it over and perhaps join him late.
4. You are in an unfamiliar city or country. You would:
   a) Orient yourself as to north, south, east and west.
   b) Let someone else worry about directions.
   c) Pay no attention.

Score
Give yourself 10 points for each of the following answers:
   1. (b)   2. (c)   3. (a)   4. (a)

Your Score
30-40: This is an excellent score on this test. Those who rate it usually react immediately in situations of danger and they waste little time mulling over unimportant daily problems. To their detriment, they may sometimes make snap judgements which they later regret.

10-20: This is a weak score and one which can lead to very real danger in times of crisis.

0: Those who rate zero are happier and better off when they follow the lead of others.

7

Would You Be A Good Detective?

> The neat art of detection seems simple when performed by a fictional character on television, but in real life an investigation involves patience, intelligence, the ability to draw conclusions, a retentive mind and keen observation.
>
> Put on your Sherlock Holmes thinking cap and see how well you do with the following questions, intelligence, the ability to draw conclusions.

Answer the following questions.
1. On the beach there are footprints of a girl leading to the ocean. They stop about 15 feet from the water's edge. "She was carried away in a Flying Saucer," the girl's mother says to you. "Otherwise, why would her footprints end here?"
   "No Flying Saucer was involved," you answer.
   How did you explain the mystery?
2. You are investigating an income-tax evasion case. "I make Rs. 100 a day, every day of the year," an executive tells you. "See, here are my books for 1964, 1965 and 1966. You will see that each year I grossed Rs. 36,500."
   "That statement alone proves that you are lying," you retort.
   On what did you base your answer?
3. After reading a story, can you remember the names of all the characters?
   Yes_____   No_____
4. Can you usually recognise a person you have met only once a long time before?
   Yes_____   No_____
5. When watching a detective TV show, do you often point out the criminal?
   Yes_____   No_____
6. Do you sometimes see people who are obviously the criminal type?
   Yes_____   No_____
7. Do you believe a statement because you read it?
   Yes_____   No_____

8. Can you, without looking back, repeat the second problem of this test?
   Yes_____   No_____
9. Are criminal tendencies hereditary?
   Yes_____   No_____
10. Are you impatient when you have to wait for a decision?
    Yes_____   No_____
11. In general, would you say you are a realist rather than being swayed by emotion?
    Yes_____   No_____
12. When a person you know well tells a lie, can you spot it?
    Yes_____   No_____
13. do you habitually carry paper, pen and make notes or lists?
    Yes_____   No_____

ANSWERS
1. The girl went into the water while the tide was high. She swam to another cove. In the meantime the tide went out leaving unmarked sand.
2. 1964, a leap year, had one extra day. Therefore, the executive's books should have listed Rs 36,600 as his income.
3. Yes
4. Yes
5. Yes.
6. No (There are no external characteristics which mark criminals).
7. No
8. Yes.
9. No (Criminologists agree that environment, not heredity, is the element that spawns criminals).
10. No
11. Yes

12. Yes
13. Yes.

Your Score

Give yourself 2 points for each correct answer.

20-26: The evidence from this test is that you would make a good detective. Perhaps, you had better warn your family and friends!

10-18: This is an average score, but probably you have no interest in ever becoming a detective, anyway. However, life will be richer if you increase your powers of observation and deduction.

0-8: You do not have the qualifications needed to become an investigator. Better be satisfied with watching detectives on television.

Would You Be A Good Witness? ⑧

> *Sometime you might be called upon to act as a witness, to report what you saw, heard or felt — from a trivial scratched fender to a major tragedy. Research shows that most of us do not register facts accurately. We see only what we think we see. However, observation, mental timing and awareness can be trained. Use this test to find out if you qualify as a good witness.*

Answer the following questions.
1. If a club meets on the Wednesday after the second Monday of each month, what are possible days of the month on which it can meet?
    11th-17th
    10th-16th
    9th-15th
    10th-17th
2. Which word does not belong in the following sets?
    a. Cod, herring, sole, whale, sardine minnow
    b. Bicycle, automobile, bus, taxi, motorcycle
    c. Rose, pansy, violet, gladiola, fern
3. Which number does not belong in each of the following sets? (*Hint:* b and c are extensions of set a)
    a. 25 16 9 100 7 36
    b. 82 65 50 16
    c. 23 14 49 34
4. Sad scenes in movies or books choke me up. (Check one)
    a. To the point of actual tears
    b. Not in the least
    c. Occasionally
5. Without looking, can you tell within 10 minutes what time it is now?
    a. I was correct.
    b. I missed.
6. I have vivid dreams. (Check one)
    a. Often
    b. Occasionally
    c. Very seldom

7. When you meet a person for the first time, can you usually remember his or her name the next day?
   a. Yes
   b. No
8. Do you feel
   a. Life has given you a fair shake?
   b. Life has been unkind to you?
   c. You have received from life just about what you deserve?

ANSWERS
1. 10-16th (1 point)
2. a. Whale (a mammal - the others are fish) (1 point)
   b. Bicycle (the others are motor driven) (1 point)
   c. Fern (the only plant that doesn't bear flowers) (1 point)
3. a. 7 (the rest are numbers squared - 25 equals 5x5; 16 equals 4x4. (3 points).
   b. 16 (the rest are numbers squared plus 1. —— 82 equals 9x9 plus 1). (3 points)
   c. 49 (the rest are numbers squared minus 2. — 23 equals 5x5-2). (3 points)
4. a-0 points; b-3; c-1
5. a-3 points; b-0
6. a-0 points; b-1; c-3
7. a-3 points; b-0
8. a-1 points; b-0; c-3

YOUR SCORE
25-28: An excellent, observant and unemotional score. You are the kind of person who, if asked a question, would

say, "I am not sure" if there was any doubt whatever in your mind.

18-24: A good score, and one that can be raised with practice in awareness. Test yourself each day with self-made questions such as, "What were the names of the cross-streets I just passed?" "What colour were his eyes?" Reconstruct a TV play in your mind, from start to finish. Or do the same with a movie.

0-17: You have a few talents to recommend you as a witness. This test has nothing to do with your success in life or your being a wonderful human being. But, it is not likely that your report on any event will be accurate.

Do You Have An Orderly Mind?

9

> *Some people are endowed with flashes of brilliance while others have more precise and orderly thought patterns, each bit of knowledge and insight falling into place like a jigsaw puzzle. While there is a place for each kind of thinking, this test will determine how precisely and orderly your thinking is.*

Test your orderly mind with each question.
1. Supply the missing word:
   Tan _____ Tin   Ton   Tun
2. Circle the number that doesn't belong in this group.
   9   18   27   32   36   45   54
3. One set of numbers is different than the rest. Can you circle the set which does not belong?
   4 5 7 4 2 8   1 1 7 2 1 9
   4 9 6 7 8   2 1 7 8 2 5 5
4. The train service became progressively worse and worse. On the first day, the 9:10 arrived at 9:25. On the second day at 9:40 and on the third day at 9:55. At what time did it arrive on the fourth day?
5. All but one of the following words have one thing in common. Circle the word that doesn't belong in the set.
   Enterprise, Tripe, Peer, Rite, Rent, Print, Pair, Rips, Enter, Nips, See, Rise, Tries, Nest
6. Can you fill in the missing numbers in sequence?
   1, 4,____, 16,____, 36,____, 64.
7. What is the missing letter on line 3?
   Rory
   Plot
   Ba__k
   Pays
8. Supply the missing letters to complete this series.
   Two W, Three H, Four O, Five __, Six __
9. One of these words does not belong in the otherwise orderly sequence. Circle it.
   Noon Let Mum Deed Poop Nun Bib Did Pop Gag

Answers

1. Ten (The middle letter is found by using each vowel, a, e, i, o, u.)
   4 points
2. 32 (In the other combinations, the sum of the two figures equals 9.)
   4 points
3. 4 9 6 7 8 (The integers in the other groups add up to 30.)
   5 points
4. 10:10 (The train ran progressively 15 minutes later each day.)
   3 points
5. Pair (All the other words can be formed by using the letters from the first word Enterprise.)
   4 points
6. 9, 25 and 49 (The progression is the square of successive numbers, 1, 2, 3, 4, 5, 6, 7 and 8.)
   5 points
7. R (Reading down the third line, the word would be Rory, the same as the top line across.)
   4 points
8. I, I (The letters you should have picked are consistently the second in the word before it.)
   3 points
9. LET (The rest of the words are spelled the same backward or forward.)
   3 points

Your Score

The highest possible score is 40.

31-35: Yours is an orderly mind which quickly ferrets out systems and sequences. You are capable of disregarding extraneous details and, step by step, you come to generalisations which are of value to you. However, you may be startled at times by people who solve problems by intuitive sense.

15-30: Your approach to problems is random rather than schematic. As a mental exercise, make up some problems of your own following the logic given in the explanations.

0-14: This is a weak score which needs to be strengthened. You make life difficult for yourself by constantly trying to put square pegs in round holes. Disregard time. Go back and carefully and thoughtfully work out each problem you missed until the sequence is perfectly clear to you.

How Well Do You Concentrate? ⑩

> *In the world of noise, interruptions and many demands, some of us become so distracted that it is difficult to concentrate on the task at hand. The art of working under pressure is one which can be developed. Use this test as a starting point to evaluate how well you are able to concentrate.*

Check out your concentration powers.
1. If FRANCE can be spelled numerically as 61811435, what countries do the groups of numbers below spell?
   a. 19161914   b.   92011225
2. a. What is the second vowel in the name of the month that follows October?
   b. What is the second letter in the name of the day which is the day that come after the day after Friday?
   c. Which letter in the word DEMAND is nearest the end of the alphabet?
3. Study the following pairs of words. One pair does not follow the pattern of the rest. Which one do you think it is?
   goat: tug   boat: tab   sad: does
   blind: did   dug: good
4. Follow the instructions given below, step by step, and see if you can fill in the missing letters in this sequence:
   _ _ S _ _ _ U _ Z _ _ _ _
   S is between N and W. Z comes between X and K. T should be placed before U. R comes after W. A comes before N. M comes after K. F should be placed to the right after M. F is the next to the last letter as you read to the right. And L finishes the line.

ANSWERS
1. A. Spain B. Italy (The letters of the alphabet are sequentially numbered: A-1; B-2, C-3, etc.)
   (10 points each)

2. A-e; B-u; C-n
   (5 points each).
3. Blind: did (In the other examples, the first letter of the first word is the same as the last letter of the last word and the last letter of the first word is the same as the first letter of the second word.)
   (25 points)
4. ANSWRTUX ZKMFL
   (15 points)

YOUR SCORE

This is a difficult test. If you scored above 50, your powers of concentration are excellent and well disciplined.

30-45: A score in this range indicates average ability to concentrate.

0-25: A score below 25 indicates a tendency to stare out of the window and fidget in chairs. It also suggests a lack of concentration with the problem at hand.

How Good Is Your Judgement? ⑪

> *Judgement involves the ability to separate fact from falsehood, truth from fancy. It also demands making an intelligent decision on the basis of known facts, without jumping to conclusions. Take this test to find out how good your judgement is.*

Test your skills with these questions.
1. Read the following two stories. The facts in them are true. Then read the statements after each story. If a statement is accurate, mark it True. If it is inaccurate, mark it False. And if you cannot tell for sure if the statement is True or False, mark it "?".

PART I

Mr. Brown returned home on the 4:30 plane. At the Baltimore airport he was unable to locate his luggage. Mrs. Brown was waiting for him and drove him home. But the luggage was located and delivered to the house at 9 that same night.

   a. Mr. Brown could not find his luggage at the Baltimore airport.
        True_____   False_____   ?___
   b. Mr. and Mrs. Brown live in Baltimore.
        True_____   False_____   ?___
   c. Mr. Brown arrived in Baltimore in the afternoon.
        True_____   False_____   ?___
   d. The missing luggage arrived at his home at 9 that night.
        True_____   False_____   ?___
   e. Mr. Brown carried a briefcase.
        True_____   False_____   ?___
   f. Mr. Brown carried a briefcase.
        True_____   False_____   ?___
   g. The luggage was mislaid at the Baltimore airport.
        True_____   False_____   ?___

PART II

On the night of his return, Mr. Brown, tired but happy, gathered the boys, John, Anthony and Paul, around him and told them about his business trip to New York. He also gave each one a present. John received a Bible, Paul got a model airplane kit and Anthony got a live turtle. He gave his wife her favourite perfume.

   a. There are five members in the Brown family.
        True_____   False_____   ?___
   b. Mr. Brown has three sons.
        True_____   False_____   ?___
   c. Anthony received a Bible.
        True_____   False_____   ?___
   d. Paul received an airplane kit.
        True_____   False_____   ?___
   e. Mrs. Brown enjoys perfumes.
        True_____   False_____   ?___

2. Do NOT use a pencil for the following questions. Make quick educated guesses.
   a. Look at these numbers. Can each one be divided evenly by 4?
      108   116   120   124   132   128
      Yes_____   No_____
   b. This is an airplane formation in a straight line. There are two jets before a jet, two jets behind a jet and one jet in the middle. What is the smallest possible number of jets?
      3___   5____   7____   9_____
   c. A man plans to build a fence along a lot that is 60 feet long. How many posts does he need if he places them 10 feet apart?
      6___   7____   10____   11_____

ANSWERS

   1. PART I (2 points for each correct answer)
      a. True
      b. ? — They could live in a town outside the city limits.

c. ? — He might have arrived on the 4:30 plane in the morning.
   d. True
   e. ? — Not mentioned in story but he might have carried a briefcase.
   f. ? — The 4:30 plane may have been early or late in arriving.
   g. ? — The luggage could have been mislaid at point of departure.

PART II (2 points for each correct answer)
   a. ? — There is no mention of the number of members in the family.
   b. ? — You cannot be sure the boys were sons. They could be nephews, visitors or neighbours.
   c. False.
   d. True.
   e. ? — This is a blanket statement. Perhaps, she enjoys only two perfumes. Her husband brought the one she likes best.

2. a. Yes (Any number is evenly divisible by 4 if the last two numbers can be divided evenly by 4.) (5 points)
   b. 3 (5 points)
   c. 7 (One at each end and 5 between) (5 points)

YOUR SCORE

30-39: A remarkable score which shows keen judgement. You evaluate clearly.

20-29: A strong score. You do not make snap judgements emotionally and without reason.

10-19: You should look before you leap and think carefully before you make a definite statement. Your judgement, as tested by these questions, indicates weaknesses which can be corrected.

Below 10: People in this range are often scattered in their thinking and are prone to hastiness.

How Well Do You Judge People? ⑫

> *Whether we realise it or not, each of us constantly judges others in order to know how to behave in the situation of confrontation. This brings up the question of accuracy when based on intuition and observation. It is not possible to be uniformly successful in estimating every quality of every person. This test presents some significant points which will help you evaluate how well you judge people.*

Answer Yes or No.
1. Do you stand by your views, even if it means damaging yourself in the eyes of someone else?
   Yes_____   No_____
2. Do you have aesthetic and/or dramatic interests?
   Yes_____   No_____
3. Do you tend to be more critical of yourself than of others?
   Yes_____   No_____
4. Would you say you have social skill?
   Yes_____   No_____
5. In evaluating someone, would you rate intelligence and integrity higher than past achievement?
   Yes_____   No_____
6. You are asked to give your opinion on a matter, but several details are not clear to you. Would you ask for an explanation even if this would mean others might regard you as uninformed or slow-witted?
   Yes_____   No_____
7. Are you always prepared to listen carefully to both sides of an argument before making up your mind?
   Yes_____   No_____
8. Do you find your friends seldom let you down?
   Yes_____   No_____
9. Do you find that you are generally dressed properly for social events?
   Yes_____   No_____
10. When watching others, do you sometimes ask yourself, "What will he or she do next?"
    Yes_____   No_____

Answers

Give yourself 2 points for each Yes answer.

Your Score

16-20: You are probably a good judge of people with whom you associate. You know that there is no such thing as a "criminal face" and in all probability you have assessed yourself so carefully that you understand others.

10-15: In all likelihood, you are often surprised and sometimes disappointed with your evaluations of others.

0-9: Testees in this range usually agree that they have little ability to judge people.

13

Can You Think Ahead?

> *You must expect to meet the unexpected since the best-laid plans of mice and men often do go astray. Needless worry is not the answer to life's many surprises. What is needed is the ability to anticipate, to select a wise, alternate course of action and to plan ahead and thus smooth rocky roads of daily living. Use this test to test how efficiently you think through future possibilities.*

Answer the following questions.
(a) When travelling, I study maps of the area.
   Yes_____   No_____
(b) Before entertaining guests in a restaurant, I find out about the hours they serve and make a reservation.
   Yes_____   No_____
(c) I have a physical and dental check-up at least once a year.
   Yes_____   No_____
(d) Before shopping, I usually make a list of what I need.
   Yes_____   No_____
(e) On a vacation, I often find that I have left at home the mates of items with me, such a shoes, cuff-links, socks.
   Yes_____   No_____
(f) I carry adequate insurance on myself, car, home, and belongings.
   Yes_____   No_____
(g) I buy things for which I later find no use.
   Yes_____   No_____
(h) I often find it necessary to borrow from friends or neighbours.
   Yes_____   No_____

ANSWERS
   A-Yes (2 points)   B-Yes (2 points)
   C-Yes (3 points)   D-Yes (3 points)
   E-No (3 points)   F-Yes (3 points)
   G-No (3 points)   H-No (3 points).

YOUR SCORE
Top score is 37 or more.

16 or more: You think and plan ahead skilfully. It is impossible to be prepared at all times for all eventualities. Life would be dull if we could always anticipate the joys and sorrows of tomorrow. However, you are not often caught with paint and no brush.

10-15: This test indicates that you are a casual person. You scold yourself for forgetting things when, in reality, you have not anticipated your needs. As mental discipline, start by making lists of shopping needs and appointments.

0-9: Life must be confusing for you. Probably those around you are often irritated. You are the kind of person who arrives at the theatre without the tickets.

Do You Have ESP?

14

> *After years of carefully controlled tests it is believed that one person out of five possesses the ability to know certain things without the use of their five physical senses: tasting, feeling, hearing, smelling and seeing. In the past many cases were ascribed to the "sixth sense" which is now called ESP — extra sensory perception. The idea of "coincidence" and "hunches" are now verified by psychological tests. This test will give you some indications about your "sixth sense".*

Answer Yes or No.
1. When the doorbell rings unexpectedly, do you sometimes know who is standing outside without first looking?
    Yes_____   No_____
2. If you wish for a letter very much, does it often arrive?
    Yes_____   No_____
3. Have you ever thought or dreamed about something that later came true?
    Yes_____   No_____
4. Have you ever felt the need to wind a stopped clock or watch, only to find the hands were at the correct time and all you had to do was wind it?
    Yes_____   No_____
5. If a friend loses something, do you sometimes awaken with knowledge of where he or she can find it?
    Yes_____   No_____
6. Have you ever stared into a glass or crystal object and seen events which later came true?
    Yes_____   No_____
7. Do you reject the idea of extrasensory perception?
    Yes_____   No_____
8. Have you ever heard a kind of "inner voice" which told you what to do?
    Yes_____   No_____
9. When the telephone rings can you sometimes greet the caller by name before they speak?
    Yes_____   No_____

ANSWERS

1. (Yes - 10 points)	2. (Yes - 10 points)
3. (Yes - 10 points)	4. (Yes - 10 points)
5. (Yes - 10 points)	6. (Yes - 10 points)
7. (No - 10 points)	8. (Yes - 10 points)
9. (Yes - 10 points).	

YOUR SCORE

70-90: This is a remarkably high score which indicates a well-developed "sixth sense". While hunches and premonitions should be carefully noted it is wise for people who rate this score also to use their knowledge and common sense.

40-60: People who fall into this category possess ESP to a degree and often can develop their intuitive instincts further if they keep their "third ear" open. Try calling the colour of cards in a deck, for example.

0-30: The average person rates in this range. When hunches come through it is more likely coincidence than true ESP. Consider yourself one of the four out of five and not the exceptional person endowed with a sixth sense.

15

Can You Untangle Problems?

> *There is seldom a day that you are not faced with a problematic situation. Sometimes life seems frustrating — as if a kitten had been playing with a ball or yarn or your fishing line were tangled. This test designed to see how you would tackle challenging situations.*

Choose one option from each question.
1. If your child were to bring a poor report card from school, you would
   a. Punish your youngster.
   b. Call the principal and complain.
   c. Make an appointment with the teacher.
2. Your feet ache. You would visit
   a. A pedicurist.
   b. A chiropodist.
   c. A chiropractor.
3. You are driving sanely, soberly and sensibly. A police car waves you to pull over. You would
   a. Keep going, knowing you have done nothing wrong.
   b. Stop and tell him you have done nothing wrong.
   c. First listen to his comments.
4. You are travelling or shopping and lose your credit cards. You would
   a. Hope for the best.
   b. Call your bank.
   c. Write, call or wire each company for which you hold a card.
5. Do you have within easy reach (without looking in a telephone book), the phone number of
   a. The fire department?
   b. The police department?
   c. Your doctor?
6. You are making a trip by plane. The stewardess gives safety instructions. You would
   a. Listen carefully.
   b. Get the jitters.

c. Pay no attention because you have heard it before.
7. You have mislaid a valuable document in your home or office. You would
   a. Become hysterical and/or angry.
   b. Tear up everything in a fast effort to find it.
   c. Quietly try to reconstruct all possibilities as to its whereabouts.
8. You cannot meet your financial obligations. You would
   a. Switch residences.
   b. Use delaying tactics by lying or making false promises.
   c. Face your creditors in an honest effort to make an adjustment.
9. A ball of string is terribly tangled. Your basic reaction would be
   a. To yank it apart.
   b. To work out the knots one by one.
   c. To cut through the knots.

ANSWERS
1. c (3 points)   2. b (1 point)
3. c (3 points)   4. c (3 points)
5. a, b, c, (3 points for each) 6. a (2 points)
7. c (2 points)   8. c (3 points)
9. b (5 points). This is important for your self-knowledge. If you strain against problems, for instance, marital rifts, the knots become tighter and more confused. If you cut, you are left with pieces.

YOUR SCORE
20-25: A remarkable score. Evidently you are patient and have what it takes to untangle problems.

15-19: A fine score. You know how to approach and solve problems. We hope you did not miss the 'emergency' point, number 6.

10-14: This is in the danger zone. You need better and more careful techniques of solving problems. Use this test as a check list.

0-9: We sincerely urge you to discuss this test with someone you trust. Your problems can be solved more easily if you approach them with logic and concentration.

Are You Logical? (16)

> *Some people have a great ability to get into a subject, to see every aspect of the problem, and then to solve it in a logical manner. Others are more disjointed in their thinking and often fail to arrive logically at relationships. This test will help you to assess your practical intelligence. It will also stimulate your thinking power.*

Attempt these logical questions and see where you stand.
1. One of the words does not logically belong in the following list:
   Fishing, rowing, dancing, fencing, running, table, mopping.
2. 4 is to 12 as 3 is to _____?
3. Which of these pairs of words is most like this sample (Forest, Tree): Cat, dog — bulb, electricity — herd, cow — fish, net.
4. When does 11 plus 3 equal 2?
5. What can you put in your right hand that you cannot put in your left hand?
6. Which one of these six things does NOT belong in the following list of mammals:
   man, elephant, hippopotamus, whale, shark, rhinoceros.

ANALYSIS
1. Table. (The rest of the words indicate activity.)
   10 points.
2. 9 (4 is one-third of 12, therefore 3 is one-third of 9).
   20 points.
3. Herd, cow. (A forest is made up of trees. Therefore a herd is made up of cows.)
   10 points.
4. Eleven o'clock plus three hours is two o'clock.
   10 points.
5. Your left elbow.
   10 points.
6. Shark.
   10 points.

YOUR SCORE
40-60: This is a high score, one to be proud of!
20-30: This is an average score. Go back and work out the problems on the basis of the explanations.
10-20: A weak score that can be improved by getting the hang of this type of test.
0: Very poor score! Wake up!

Do You Think Logically? (17)

> *In research studies it has been found that there is less correlation between intelligence and the ability to think logically than one would assume. Many people who rated high on IQ tests failed to solve the problem situations.*

The following questions will test your ability to think situations through in logical sequence.
1. A traffic survey was made in six towns to determine which had the most cars. From the information given below, put the towns in order according to the number of cars.
    a) Newport had three towns which topped it for the number of cars.
    b) Centerville had more cars than any of the others.
    c) Pumpkin Center had 1,500 fewer cars than the rest.
    d) Milltown came next to Newport with 500 fewer cars.
    e) Blairsville had 200 more cars than Newport.
    f) Seatown had a few less cars than Centerville.
2. A clock face shows the time is 20 minutes past seven. If this time were seen in a mirror, what would the clock read?
3. What two groups of letters would logically follow these?
    AZA BXB CUC DQD ???   ???
4. Try your sleuthing ability on this case.
    A house was entered and robbed. The police arrived immediately. There was every indication that the thieves were experts. They had obviously enjoyed themselves for there were empty cans of food, a half-eaten apple, and scraps of bread littered the floor. But the police could find no fingerprints or footprints. How did the police chief track the robbers down?

Answers

1. b (Centerville)
   f (Seatown)
   e (Blairsville)
   a (Newport)
   b (Milltown)
   c (Pumpkin Center)
   5 points
2. Twenty minutes to five
   5 points
3. ELE, FFF. (The first and last letters in each set are obviously a normal progression of the alphabet. The middle letter, starting from the back of the alphabet, jumps one letter more in each set.)
   20 points.
4. Taking the only bit of evidence, the police had moulds made of the tooth marks on the bread and apple. Feeling certain the thieves were professional, they threw out a dragnet for everyone in their files with past robbery records and hauled them in for dental examinations. One man was found whose teeth were obviously those on the half-eaten apple and he confessed and named his accomplices.
   15 points

Your Score

30-40: An exceptional score! Outstanding too, because you can think visually, mathematically and abstractly.
10-20: The average range.
0-5: Below average. You lack the ability to think out complex problems. Never mind, you may improve if you put your mind to it.

Are You Ingenious? ⬜18

> *Ingenuity is a mysterious quality which separates the mediocre and the brilliant. Psychologists find it difficult to define, but see it generally as the ability to extend ideas in unusual ways. This test will help you discover if you are able to do just that — extend ideas.*

Discover your ingenuity with the following questions.
1. A moving van which was 11 feet 15 inches high could not go through an underpass marked as 11 feet 13 inches. The police arrived and pondered over the problem.
   The driver was frantic, fearing he would have to retrace his route and drive miles out of his way.
   A 12-year-old boy watched with interest, thought the problem through and suggested a workable answer.
   What was his solution so that the truck could proceed through the underpass?
2. What is the next number in this series?
   1, 1, 2, 6, ____.
3. If HOUSE were spelled EHOSU, how would you spell
   JAPAN?
   PLANE?
   REFER?
4. A wife in a farm sent her husband to a spring with instructions to bring back 1 gallon (4 quarts) of water.
   The husband had only two unmarked cans. One held 3 quarts. The other held 5 quarts. He returned with exactly 1 gallon of water. How did he do it?

ANSWERS
Give yourself one point for each correct answer.
1. The boy suggested that the truck driver deflate the tires.

2. 24 (Each number is multiplied by one more: one, two, three and four).
3. NJAAP, EPLNA, RREEF (The letters are shuffled so that the last letter becomes the first letter and the resulting last two letters are transposed.)
4. First the husband filled the 5-quart jar. From it he filled the 3-quart jar which he emptied. He then poured the 2 quarts left in the 5-quart jar into the 3-quart jar. He refilled the 5-quart jar and poured enough (1-quart) to fill the 3-quart jar. He had exactly 4 quarts left in the 5-quart jar.

Your Score
All correct: An outstanding score! You can project ideas.
0-1 correct: This is a low score but does not mean that you necessarily lack intelligence.

19

How Creative Are You?

> *Creativity demands imagination, the ability to improvise, the courage to combine known facts or things to create something new. The following problems will give you an inkling of how creative you are.*

Answer the following questions.
1. Study the following sample:
   Sunset Red Blook Accident Ambulance
   Through word association, each word leads to the next. Can you supply words to fill the following blanks? (The number of dashes hint the number of letters.)
   a) CHURCH _ _ _ _ _ _ _ _
      _ _ _ _ LEAVES
   b) OCEAN _ _ _ _ _ _ _ _ _
      _ _ _ _ UNITED STATES
   c) BIRD _ _ _ _ _ _ _ _ _ _
      SHINE
2. On an outing with two boys, you are faced with the problem of crossing a lake in a rowboat. But the rowboat can carry only 200 lbs. You weigh 200 lbs., and each boy weighs 100 lbs. What can you do?
3. Answer the following questions by circling True of False:
   a. I have never tried my hand at writing poetry.
      True_____   False_____
   b. I always keep my furniture in the same position.
      True_____   False_____
   c. I leave fads like mini-skirts or double-coloured pants for others to wear.
      True_____   False_____
   d. I prefer factual books to fiction.
      True_____   False_____
   e. I prefer others to solve my problems for me.
      True_____   False_____

f. (For women) I always follow a recipe when I cook.
   True_____   False_____
g. (For men) I buy tools, furniture, and machines only if they are pre-assembled.
   True_____   False_____
h. I am depressed if my plans do not work out on the first try.
   True_____   False_____
i. I do not see shapes in clouds or in burning logs in a fireplace.
   True_____   False_____
j. Classical music leaves me cold.
   True_____   False_____
k. I abandon a project if I do not have all necessary items.
   True_____   False_____

ANSWERS
1. Possible answers: Church, Pews, Wood, Trees, Leaves; Ocean, Waves, Flag, United States; Bird, Blue, Sky, Sun and Shine. If your answers are different but still make sense, give yourself 3 points for each line of association answer.
2. Very simple. You asked the two boys to row across the lake. One stayed on the far side while the other rowed back for you. You then rowed alone to the far side and sent the boy there to row back for his friend at the starting point. They came back to the far side together.
   5 points
3. Give yourself 3 points for each False answer (possible total - 30)

YOUR SCORE

35-44: You are definitely in the creative bracket, being able to both see and to act. You are capable of improvising, the sort of person who, lacking a hammer will pound a nail with a shoe.

15-34: You do not create equally well in all fields, but are capable of working out answers when the need is there. Because original ideas and projects are personally satisfying, you might consider giving up some of your golf games or bridge sessions and taking a course in painting, music or literature.

0-14: Creativity is not your strong point. Better learn to read directions with accuracy. Do not despair, however, for you are probably conservative and will likely never get into trouble by unwise experimentation.

Are You Observant?

20

> *There is a great difference between seeing and observing. When your eyes take in a scene, do they record details or just harvest an over all impression? This test will give you some indications about your power of observation.*

Study the drawing given below for two minutes. Then cover the drawing and answer the following questions.

1. The fire occurred on the ground floor.
   True_____   False_____
2. The fire occurred in a building at Maple and Fourth.
   True_____   False_____
3. According to the clock the firemen are at the blaze shortly after three.
   True_____   False_____
4. The first name of the jeweller on the ground level is William.
   True_____   False_____
5. All rooms in the building are rented.
   True_____   False_____
6. The fire hose shown in the picture is not connected to the hydrant.
   True_____   False_____
7. The three stores shown at street level are a butcher, a baker and a candlestick maker.
   True_____   False_____
8. The car which is help up by the fire is an open convertible.
   True_____   False_____
9. The street address of the bakery store is 364.
   True_____   False_____
10. The bakery store has a sign in the window advertising fresh apple pie.
    True_____   False_____
11. The meat market has a sign in the window advertising fresh ham.
    True_____   False_____
12. A dog is sitting on the sidewalk.
    True_____   False_____
13. Only one window has curtains which can be seen from the street.
    True_____   False_____
14. There are 21 people shown in the drawing.
    True_____   False_____

15. Three firemen are shown in the drawing.
    True_____   False_____
16. The woman in the window is calling for assistance.
    True_____   False_____
17. Two of the onlookers are wearing hats.
    True_____   False_____
18. The sidewalk is roped off.
    True_____   False_____

ANSWERS

1. (False - 1 point)
2. (False - 5 points)
3. (True - 2 points)
4. (True - 2 points)
5. (False - 5 points)
6. (True - 2 points)
7. (False - 1 point)
8. (False - 2 points)
9. (True - 10 points)
11. (True - 5 points)
12. (False - 1 point)
13. (True - 5 points)
14. (True - 10 points)
15. (True - 2 points)
16. (True - 1 point)
17. (True - 5 points)
18. (True - 1 point).

YOUR SCORE

50-62: This is an excellent score and shows keen powers of observation. You seem to possess the unique ability to assess the total situation and then to see and remember such easy-to-overlook things as street numbers, signs and the approximate number of people around them.

20-49: An average score which can be improved. In all probability you looked at the action, in this case the fire, and read the bakery sign.

But most likely you did not read the butcher sign or the street sign.

0-19: This is a weak score. If you wish to improve your powers of observation, one method is to start looking into the eyes of others. At the end of each day, list the colours of eyes you have seen. As your observation grows, draw a picture of the shape of those eyes.

Are they oval? Slanted?
Do they have "crows feet" around them?
Are they heavy-lidded?
You will be astonished how much you can learn by using this technique.

21

How Good Is Your Visual Memory?

> *Over five senses — touch, hearing, smell, sight and taste — feed information to the brain which is recorded as memory. Psychological laboratory tests have proven that an individual may have one sense developed to a higher degree than the others. Learning to spell correctly is an example. Some people need to look at words. Others need to spell it out loud, while others write it several times until the "feeling" of the letters is firm in their minds. This test will evaluate only your visual memory.*

Study the cartoon. Take as long as you like. Do not read the questions in the test until after you've finished looking over the cartoon. Then cover the cartoon with your hand or a piece of paper. And answer the questions — but do not peek at the cartoon again.

1. The angry customer in the cartoon is shaking his (check one)
   a. Right hand _____   b. Left hand _____
2. The restaurant has a plant in a container.
   a. Yes_____   b. No_____
3. The waiter who is being scolded holds a tray in his hand.
   a. Yes_____   b. No_____
4. The cartoon shows:
   a. Two men____
   b. Three men____
   c. Four men____
5. One man is smoking a pipe.
   a. Yes_____   b. No_____
6. The angry guest is wearing a tie which is
   a. Solid colour____
   b. Striped____
   c. A bow tie____
7. The angry customer has on the sleeve of his coat
   a. Three buttons.
   b. No buttons.
   c. One button.
8. The waiter who is being scolded by the customer has a bushy head of hair.
   a. Yes_____   b. No_____
9. There is no glass on the customer's table.
   a. Yes_____   b. No_____
10. The customer's tablecloth is
    a. Plaid.
    b. Flowered.
    c. Plain.
11. The customer's trousers are
    a. White.
    b. Black.
    c. Not shown.

12. The cartoonist drew two ears on
    a. One man.
    b. Two men.
    c. Three men.
13. The cartoonist drew the customer sitting in a chair.
    a. True____   b. False____
14. The waiter who is being scolded has his jacket
    a. Buttoned.
    b. Unbuttoned____
15. Each waiter holds something in his left hand.
    a. True____   b. False____

ANSWERS

1.	a-3	2.	a-5
3.	a-3	4.	c-10
5.	a-10	6.	b-10
7.	b-10	8.	b-3
9.	b-7	10.	c-3
11.	c-3	12.	a-10
13.	b-3	14.	b-10
15.	a-10		

YOUR SCORE

83-100: This score indicates a very high visual memory. Those who fall into this range often say, "I remember the face, but I can't remember the name by which we were introduced."

50-82: Most people seem to fall into this rating. Being versatile with all senses, they use many ways of learning. (If you want to make this test more interesting, ask someone to describe the picture to you and take the test again. This will challenge your sense of hearing. Or, talk to yourself about the picture and then repeat the test. But, remember — no peeking!)

20-49: This score does not indicate a high degree of visual memory. You can improve it if you wish by using your eyes and then writing down the things you see. Instead of "counting sheep at night," visualise three objects in your living quarters and then go back later and check for the accuracy of your observation.

0-19: A low score. If your aim is to improve your visual memory, follow all the suggestions given above and practise visualising things.

Can You Follow Directions?

22

Today's fast-moving, inventive world is filled with directions. There are directions on the package which explains how to open a box of crackers and directions with diagrams explaining how to build a boat. There are directions which tell how to assemble something and some are a bit confusing. This test will help you evaluate your ability to follow directions.

1. Study the diagram. Then follow the directions given in A through F and write down all your answers.

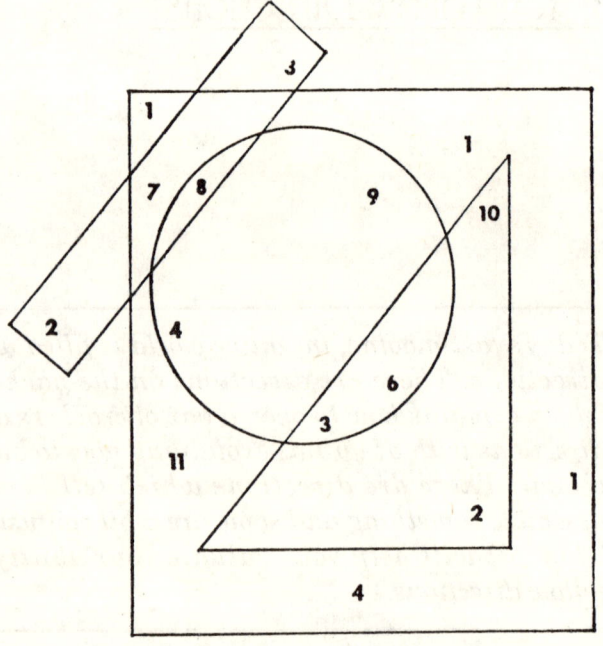

A. Add all the numbers in the square which are not in the circle, triangle or rectangle. Write the sum you got here._____
B. Reverse the sum you have just written. Write the new number here._____
C. Add all the numbers which appear in the triangle. Write the sum here._____
D. Subtract your answer C from your answer B. Write the difference here._____

E. If your answer to A is larger than your answer to D, write down an X here._____
   F. Circle each 1 in the diagram. How many circles have you made altogether?_____
2. Many foreign countries present safety and directional signs in a very practical form. What do these directive signs (A through F, below) tell you?

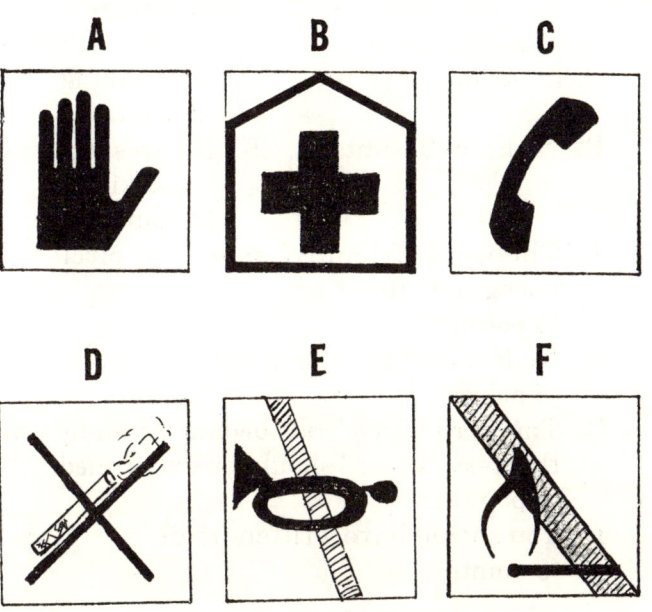

3. Keeping in mind the 5 minute time limit, follow these directions as quickly as you possibly can:
   A. If the word "friendly" appears in this paragraph, circle it.
   B. If California is on the West Coast, leave the word "pumpkin" as it is. If the opposite is true, underline all the P's.
   C. If the word "circle" has been used more than once in this test, then underline the word "Coast."

D. If a woman is a female, write the word "mail" here____

ANSWERS
1. A. 18 (5 points)   B. 81 (3 points)
   C. 21 (5 points)   D. 60 (5 points)
   E. No X (5 points)   F. There are six 1's.
                           (Note two 1's in 11.)
                           (3 points)
2. A. Stop (2 points)   B. Hospital (2 points)
   C. Telephone (2 points)   D. No smoking
                                 (2 points)
   E. No horn (2 points)   F. No fires (no smoking,
                                 no cooking)
                                 (2 points).
3. A. The word "friendly" should be circled. First paragraph, first line.
      (5 points)
   B. No P should be underlined.
      (5 points)
   C. The word "circle" has been used many times in this test. "Coast" should be underlined.
      (5 points)
   D. You should have written "mail."
      (5 points).

YOUR SCORE
If you followed the directions which require a 5-minute time limit for this test, your ability to carry out instructions should be as follows:
54-58: This is an excellent score! You read words, symbols and pictures with care and you definitely can follow directions.
30-53: This is an average rating. Probably you can follow directions better when the hands of the clock are not moving against you.

0-29: This is low score. Take hope, however, for you may be one of the intuitive people who do not have to read directions to get things done.

Can You Solve Problems? **23**

> *Many things in life take a lot of thinking about. Fast action is not necessarily the correct action, even in cases of emergency. Snap judgements, say the psychological experts, are hazardous. To take this test do not pressure yourself. Take all the time you want to study each problem. Enjoy stretching your brain.*

Answer these questions.
1. You have five pieces of chain. Each piece has links, as shown in the drawing below.

   You wish to have them welded together to form a single chain.
   The blacksmith tells you that he charges Rs. 5 to cut a link and Rs. 10 for welding it together.
   "Fine," you say. "The whole job will cost Rs. 60."
   "No," says the honest blacksmith. "I can do the job for only Rs. 45."
   How does the blacksmith maintain his prices and still do the job for Rs. 45?
2. Place the numbers 1 to 9 in the nine blank-squares so that the sum of the figures in each row - vertical, horizontal and diagonal — is 15.

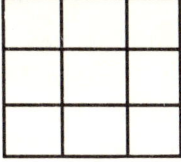

3. A geographical survey was made to determine how a number of towns ranked in altitude. From the

information given in the next paragraph, list the towns in order, highest above sea level first: "Balmouth is higher than Carden, but lower than Telcomb, which is lower than Denton. Fenland is higher than Denton."

4. You are to supply the two missing pair of letters in the following series:
   BE   CF   DG   _____;   _____.

5. The following three squares (at left) are made with 10 toothpicks. Which two toothpicks can you cover with your fingers to leave two squares of the same size?

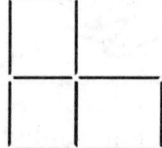

Answers

Give yourself 20 points for each correct answer.

1. The blacksmith cut all three links of the first piece. Then he used them to join the other pieces.
2. The numbers should be placed as shown below.

8	1	6
3	5	7
4	9	2

3. Starting with the highest town: Fenland, Denton, Telcomb, Balmouth, Carden.
4. EH, FI (In this sequence, each letter moves forward one time in the alphabet).
5. By covering the two toothpicks which form the lower left-hand corner, you leave two squares of the same size.

YOUR SCORE

80-100: This is an excellent score which shows that you can think about the problem at hand. It is unlikely that you dash in all directions. Some of your friends may consider you too logical and a bit slow in making decisions, but the chances are extremely high that you will make the correct choice in solving almost any of your problems.

40-60: Under psychological laboratory conditions, this is an average score.

0-20: This poor score is made by persons who are unable to concentrate or to solve problems. People in this category often claim they "have other things to do." But if they are given some good reason to try harder, they can usually improve their scores.

24

How Fast Can You See Things?

> *This quiz will help you assess your ability to visualise things quickly and to concentrate. Each of these talents can be improved. If you find any of the problems given in this test difficult or impossible to solve, serious study of those problems will, in itself, be a productive brain exercise.*

Answer these questions.
1. Two of the 15 horses' heads (right) are identical in every respect. Can you find the two that are exactly alike?

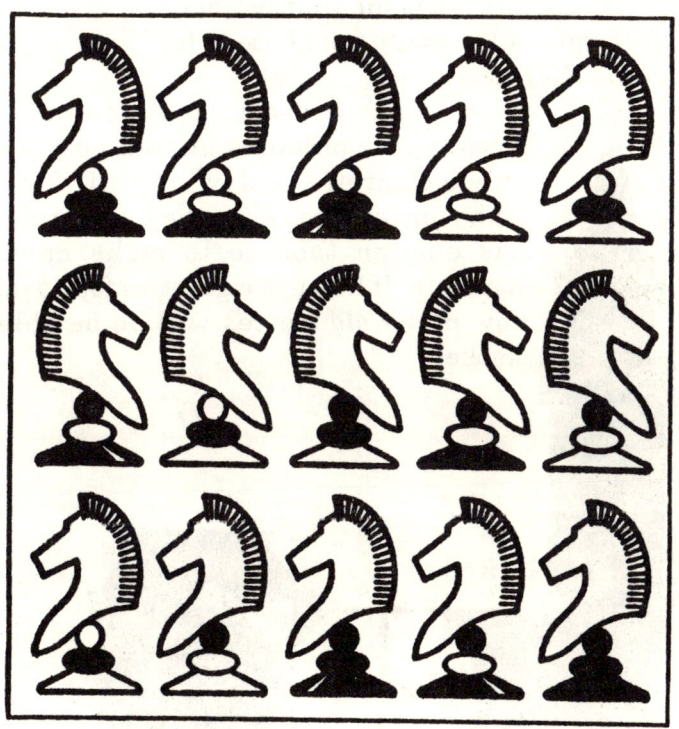

2. Which one of these three geometric figures (below) can be drawn in one continuous stroke without retracing any lines?

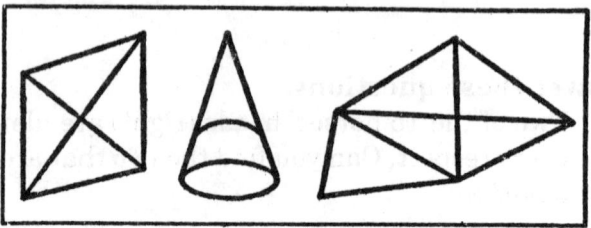

3. Using the portion of the church (below) marked 100 feet as the basis for your estimation, what is the height of the tower from base to top? Take a guess, do NOT measure.

4. A man decides to cut down on his smoking. He promises himself he will buy only 5 cigarettes a day but will keep the stubs for tobacco. When he has 5 stubs he has enough tobacco to make another cigarette. If he buys cigarettes for 25 days, how many cigarettes will he be able to smoke?

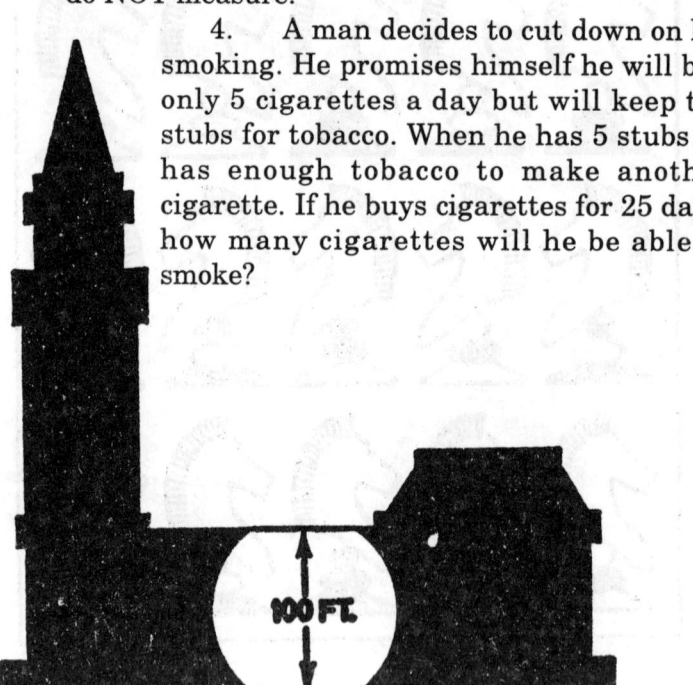

5. Here you must add the two words given to make a new word that's missing. For example: Proper plus flower equals primrose.

(A) Vehicle plus family animal equals something on the floor
(B) Male plus time of life equals to administer.

Answers
1. The identical horses' heads are at the far right top row and the first head at the far left in the bottom row.
   (20 points for correct answer.)
2. Only the geometric figure at the far left can be drawn in one continuous line. See the diagram below.
   (20 points.)
3. The tower's height is 375 feet. If you guessed 350 or 400 feet you have still made a good estimate.
   (20 points).
4. 156 cigarettes. In 25 days he will buy 125 cigarettes. From the stubs, he will be able to make 25 cigarettes. From the stubs of these he can make another 5 cigarettes. From the stubs of the last 5 he can make another cigarette.
   (20 points).
5. (A) carpet (10 points); (B) manage (10 points).

Your Score
80-100: This is an exceptionally high score regardless of how long it required you to take the test. Both your Eye-Q and I.Q. show ability.

30-70: This is an average score. Very often testees who fall into this bracket are unable to concentrate or are distracted by other things. They usually do much better if they have time and the willingness to work on such problems as those given in this test.

0-20: Testees in this range need to improve their powers of concentration and their ability to see. It is a proven fact that I.Q. can be expanded by mental exercise and the Eye-Q can be trained by careful observation.

25

Do You See Details?

> *Visual perception varies widely among individuals. Some people take in the total scene while others are quick to notice crooked stocking seams or sagging pictures on the wall. In many respects, this variance of ability to see is a good thing because it provides different aptitudes which are important to the many different types of work required by modern living. This test will help you evaluate whether you have "extensive" perception (seeing the total) or "intensive" perception (seeing details).*

Answer these questions and find out whether you are observant.
1. The following sentence is often used in typing and penmanship classes. What is unusual about it? The quick brown fox jumps over the lazy dog.
2. Carefully read the words in each of the triangles (bottom, right). What do they say?

3. A husband designed this door (right) for his house. "It is more than just a door," he told his wife. There are more than a dozen letters hidden in the design. Can you find them if you look for conventional capital letters made up of straight lines?

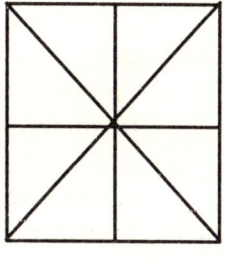

4. The following paragraph is unusual in one respect. Can you discover why?
Can you find out what is unusual about this paragraph? It looks so ordinary that you might think nothing is wrong with it. Nothing is wrong but it is unusual. Look at it; study it: Think about it and you may find out. Who knows? Good luck!

5. Study each row of ovals (left) carefully. There is a logical sequence in each. What shapes and how many should be in the last, empty oval?

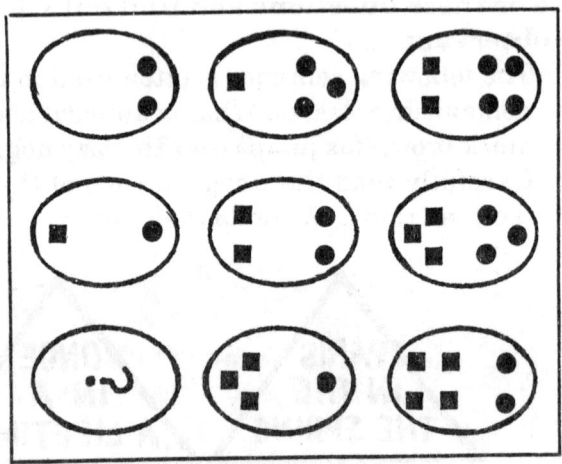

ANSWERS
1. The sentence contains each letter of the alphabet. If you answered correctly, give yourself 4 points.
2. Did you spot the repeated words? "Paris in the *the* spring; Once in a *a* lifetime."
   6 points if you got both correct.
3. The letters in the door design are: E, F, H, I, K, L, M, N, T, V, W, X, Y, Z.
   2 points for each letter you found.
4. The paragraph is unusual because it is without the most used letter in the alphabet, "e".
   20 points.

5. There should be two black squares at the bottom of the last oval. In each line there is a pattern. The top dots decrease by one each time and the squares increase by one each time.
30 points.

YOUR SCORE
80-88: This is an exceptional score. People who rank in this bracket have the potential to be excellent editors, technicians and scientists. Associates and friends may consider these people to be too involved with details. "Can't see the forest for the trees."
50-78: An average score. Testees tend to be concerned both with details and the overall picture of life around them.
0-48: This score is often made by those who have difficulty in concentrating. In all probability they have something they think is more important on their minds.

26

Are You Sharp-Witted?

> *Many psychologists say man has five wits: common sense, imagination, fantasy, estimation and memory. To this they add the five senses as our channels of learning. When these 10 human assets are alert and trained, the mind and the body combine to produce nature's most observant creature. This test will help you evaluate some of your native talents and the extent to which you have trained them.*

Have a go at these and test your wits.
1. If your men, A, B, C, and D, were standing with their backs together at the South Pole and each began to walk directly ahead, in what direction would each be going? A____, B____, C____, D____.
2. Work the cross-number problem as you would a crossword puzzle, filling in the blank squares both horizontally and vertically. For instance, top row horizontal: 4 x 1 - 2 = 2

4	x		-		=2
+		x		x	
	x		+		=5
-		+		+	
x		-		=1	
=5		=4		=9	

3. The name of my favourite cartoonist is
   a. _____
   b. Don't know_____.
4. The numeral 10 on the back face of a Rs. 10 note occurs in all four corners. Yes____ No_____
5. How many spokes are there in the wheel on the flag of India?_____

ANSWERS
1. Each man, being at the South Pole, would necessarily be walking north, the only direction you

can go when you are exactly at the South Pole. (4 points).
2. Horizontal Vertical
    4 x 1 - 2 = 2   4 + 3 - 2 = 5
    3 x 1 + 2 = 5   1 x 1 + 3 = 4
    2 x 3 - 5 = 1   2 x 2 + 5 = 9
   (2 points for each correct line).
3. If you knew the name of the cartoonist, 5 points.
4. If you knew without looking, 4 points.
5. 24 spokes. 3 points.

Your Score

20-28: This score indicates well-sharpened wits. Your memory recall is outstanding as well as your ability to estimate. You can very likely put things in their proper place and in their proper order. You are observant and curious about things around you.

14-19: This is an average score on this test. It indicates efficiency but you shut out some details, possibly because they are things which do not interest you. Try to broaden the scope of your interests.

7-13: Your wits are with you and could easily be sharpened to the keenest level. It takes both work and knowledge to keep mind, soul and body intact and in good working order to produce really keen wits.

0-6: Your scoring on this test indicates that you can improve yourself. Keep looking, keep remembering, keep thinking. Practice in observing things will greatly sharping your outlook and create a more alert overall mental attitude.

27

Can You Think in 3 Dimensions?

> *Psychologists agree that there are many kinds of intelligence. This test, will help you to assess your ability to think in terms of three dimensions. This requires a specific type of intelligence, so if you do not do well, don't be too concerned because your intelligence may be stronger in other ways.*

Test your skills.

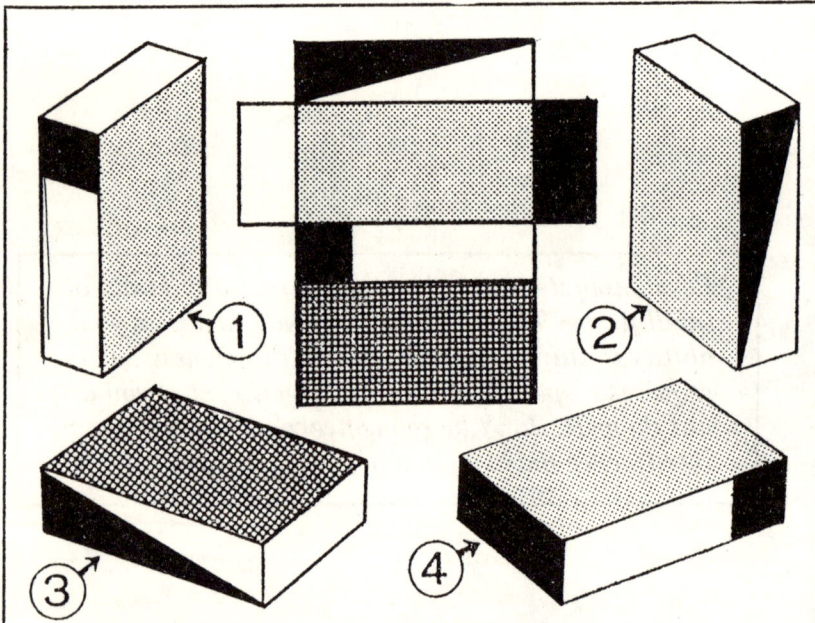

Problem 1: Each of these four numbered boxes is made out of one flat piece of cardboard like that shown opened out in center drawing. Which box (1, 2, 3 or 4) is made from that center piece?

Problem 1: Each of these four numbered boxes is made out of one flat piece of cardboard like that shown opened out in centre drawing. Which box (1, 2, 3, or 4) is made from that centre piece?

Problem 2: Which two boxes above were made from the flat piece of cardboard shown below?

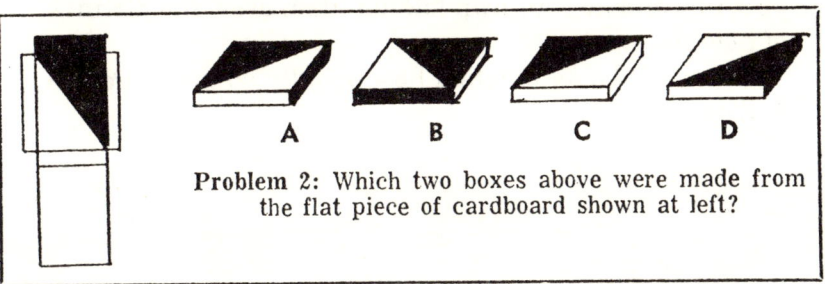

Problem 2: Which two boxes above were made from the flat piece of cardboard shown at left?

Problem 3: Which cylinder (A, B, C or D) was formed from the flat cardboard shown below?

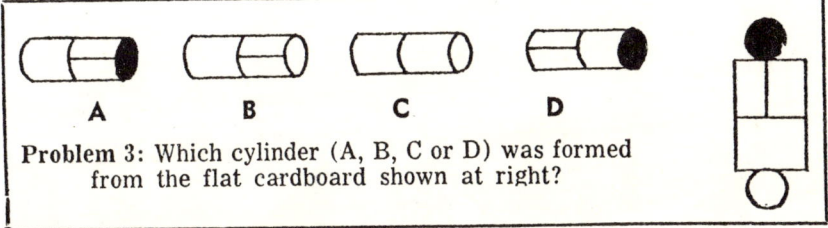

Problem 3: Which cylinder (A, B, C or D) was formed from the flat cardboard shown at right?

Answers

Give yourself 20 points for each correct solution.
Problem 1: (box 1)
Problem 2: (boxes "C" and "D")
Problem 3: (cylinder "A").

Your Score

60 points: Those who rate this score are excellent in fields which require spatial vision, such as architects, sculptors, designers, manufacturers and packers.

40 points: This is above average, if you adhered to the two-minute limit in answering the problems.
20 points: Most testees fall into this bracket. Problem 3 was most often answered correctly.
No points: If you wish to improve your ability to think three-dimensionally, make some rough cardboard patterns and do your own folding, then draw the pictures of how they look.

You will be astonished how rapidly your perception will develop!

28

How Great Is Your Brain Power?

> *Many people get along very well in this world by being charming but "not too bright". Adaptability, willingness and hard work achieve often more than brain power without endeavor. But, if brain-power is added to the other ingredients, those persons are almost always sure fire successes. This test is devised to test visual and mathematical abilities. Your ability to read this test and to understand the vocabulary used are also tests of your intelligence.*

Allow yourself 15 minutes to complete these problems.

1. One of the five numbered geometric figures is shown in the top left box from the other side. Is it 1, 2, 3, 4 or 5?

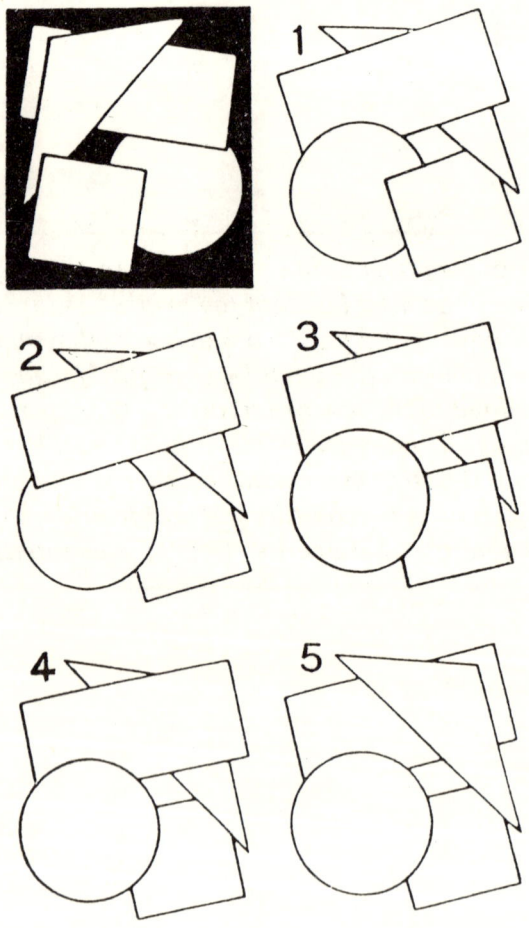

2. Answer these questions about the diagram below:

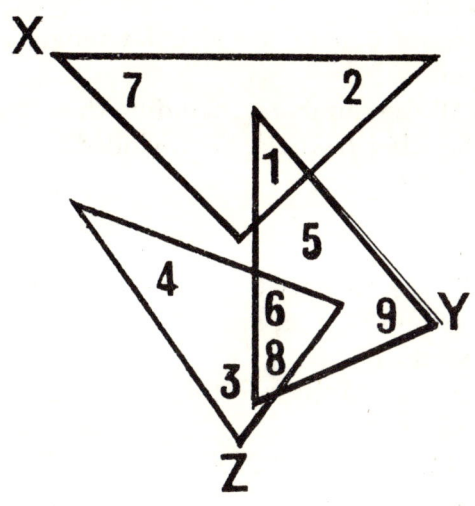

a. What is the sum of the numbers in triangle Z *only?* _____
b. What is the sum total of *all* the numbers in triangle Y? _____
c. What is the sum total of the numbers in X, Y, and Z which appear in *only* one triangle? _____
d. What is the sum of the numbers which appear in *two* of the triangles at the same time? _____
3. See if you can figure this out!
   B is to F as M is to _____.
4. Underline two of the following words which contain *exactly* the same letters:
   CHARTS   SCYTHE   STARCHY
   TEACH   CHESTY   CHEATS

SOLUTIONS
1. Geometric figure 4
   20 points
2. a. 7 (note: 6 and 8 are also in triangle Y)
   10 points
   b. 29 (All the numbers, including those which appear in the other triangle, are included.)
   10 points
   c. 30
   10 points
   d. 15 (There are only three numbers which appear in two triangles: 1, 6, and 8.)
   10 points
3. Q (Interval of three letters)
   5 points
4. SCYTHE and CHESTY
   5 points

ANALYSIS
50-70: This is a remarkably high score *if* you kept within the time limit. It indicates great brain power and mental ability. If you arrived at this score but took a longer time to work out the solutions, pat yourself on the back for your diligence which, with your intelligence, will take you far in life.

20-40: A good score which would indicate an above average intelligence. Because no one of us stretched his brain power to its limits, you can probably go farther.

0-15: You are letting your brain power idle. It was once thought that intelligence is an inherent quality, like the nose on your face.

Do You Use Your Brain Power?

(29)

> *Many people get along very well by being charming and "not too bright". Adaptability, willingness and hard work often achieve more than brain power without endeavour. But, if brain power is added to other ingredients, that person is almost always a sure-fire success. This test will help you estimate your ability to classify relationships. These types of problems are often given in intelligence tests. Getting the "hang" of them may be helpful to you in the future.*

Give 2 minutes for each problem.
1. Look at the figure below and study the placement of the black-and-white halves of the circles in the top row. Then study the placement in the middle row and compare with the top row. How do you shade in the 3 empty circles on the bottom row to fit the sequential pattern?

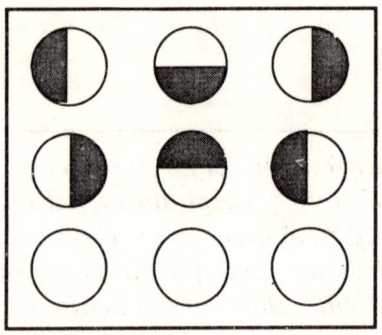

2. B is to F as M is to _____.
3. Here are seven words. First find the simple code. Which jumbled word does not belong with the rest? sinnet; gnimmiws; yekcoh; llabtoof; gnitaks; notnimdab; gnihsaw
4. Which design does not belong with the rest?

 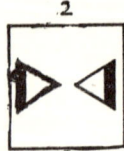 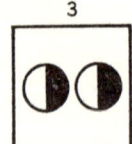  

5. Which one of the numbered squares belongs in the dotted square fourth from the left?

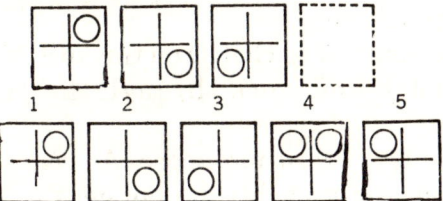

Answers and Scoring

1.

   There is a pattern here. The black half of the circle moves counter-clockwise 90 degrees each time and the first circle in each row is the same as the last one in the line above.
   (20 points)
2. Q - There is an interval of three letters.
   (10 points)
3. The code is that the words are spelled backwards. gnishaw (washing) does not belong since the rest are sports.
   (10 points)
4. Design 3 does not belong. In the other examples the pattern of black and white are opposite while in 3 the pattern of black and white are the same.
   (20 points)
5. Square 5. The circle in the first three squares moves clockwise one quarter in each square.
   (20 points)

Analysis

(Highest possible score on this test is 80)

70-80: This is an excellent score if you adhered to the time limit. You obviously are observant and use your brain power. Do not be self-content, however, for this is a relatively easy test. Find some test books which will challenge you further.

40-60: Rate yourself as GOOD on this test. You will profit if you go back and work through the problems you missed.

20-30: This is a below par score. As was stated in the introduction, you probably did not get the "hang" of the problems. Try again and, if you still do not understand ask someone to explain to you in their own words.

0-10: Sorry, but you will have to give yourself a POOR on these problems. What was your problem? Inability to read the instructions correctly? Unwillingness to concentrate? You can find your own cure if you wish.

Can You Identify Forms?

30

> Psychologists and educators agree that one of the greatest problems of attempting to evaluate abilities, aptitudes and intelligence lies in language. Those who have been educationally deprived, or who come from an environment where a language is used that is not the one used in the test, often fail to exhibit their true mental worth. This test will test your talents in identifying forms.

Test your potential to identify forms.

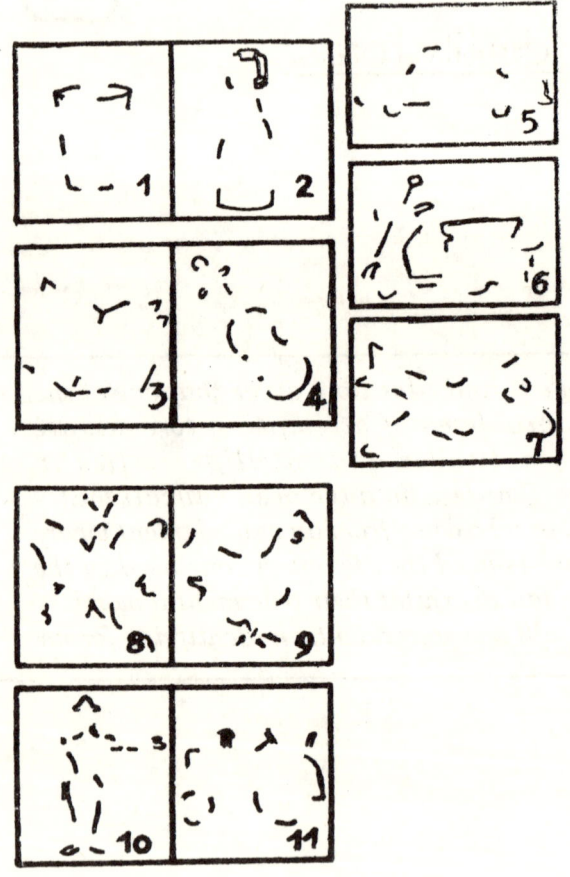

Below you will find eleven broken pictures. You have only two minutes to identify as many of the objects as you can. Write in answers in the box provided.

1. _____
2. _____
3. _____
4. _____
5. _____
6. _____
7. _____
8. _____
9. _____
10. _____
11. _____

ANSWERS

1. Glass   2. Bottle   3. Book
4. Violin   5. Car   6. Scooter
7. Airplane 8. Butterfly 9. Chicken
10. Policeman (or hitch-hiker)   11. Tractor.

Give yourself
1 point each for 1 through 4,
2 points each for 5 through 7,
3 points each for 8 through 11.

YOUR SCORE

15-22: This is a very fine score, provided you kept within the time limit. It indicates a good, functioning I.Q. and a keen sense of observation.

10-14: People who are in this bracket can consider themselves average. It is fun to expand our brains and observation powers by making your own broken drawings of familiar forms which are around us every day.

0-9: A rating which is below par for a visual test. However, many people who rate this score excel in other abilities.